j363.1 Day, James.
DAY
The Hindenburg
tragedy

Copy 1

$10.90   h q

Public Library

1 Van Ingen Drive
Webster, NY 14580
716-872-7075

GREAT DISASTERS

THE HINDENBURG TRAGEDY

James Day

Illustrated by Nik Spender

The Bookwright Press
New York · 1989

Great Disasters

The Chernobyl Catastrophe
The Hindenburg Tragedy
The Eruption of Krakatoa
The Fire of London

The Destruction of Pompeii
The San Francisco Earthquake
The Space Shuttle Disaster
The Sinking of the Titanic

First published in the
United States in 1989 by
The Bookwright Press
387 Park Avenue South
New York, NY 10016

First published in 1988 by
Wayland (Publishers) Limited
61 Western Road, Hove
East Sussex BN3 1JD

© Copyright 1988 Wayland (Publishers) Limited

Front cover *7:21 p.m.: The* Hindenburg *as it catches fire on May 6, 1937 at Lakehurst, New Jersey.*

Words that are printed in **bold** the first time they appear in the text are explained in the glossary on page 30.

Library of Congress Cataloging-in-Publication Data

Day, James
    The Hindenburg tragedy/ by James Day:
illustrated by Nik Spender.
       p.   cm. — (Great disasters)
    Bibliography: p.
    Includes index.
    Summary: Describes the development and launching of the
famous airship and its disastrous accident at an airfield in
New Jersey.
    ISBN 0-531-18238-X
    1. Hindenburg (Airship) — Juvenile literature. 2. Aeronautics –
Accidents — 1937 — Juvenile literature. [1. Hindenburg (Airship)
2. Airships. 3. Aeronautics — Accidents.] I. Spender, Nik, ill.
II. Title. III. Series.
TL659.H5D38 1989
363.1'2492 – dc19
                                88-19879
                                        CIP
                                        AC

Phototypeset by Oliver Dawkins Ltd, Burgess Hill, West Sussex
Printed in Italy by G. Canale & C.S.p.A, Turin

CONTENTS

EYEWITNESS

On the evening of May 6, 1937, the radio announcer Herbert Morrison was waiting at Lakehurst airfield in New Jersey. The world's largest airship, the *Hindenburg*, was about to land. It was twelve hours late. Stiff headwinds and rain had slowed its journey across the Atlantic from Frankfurt in Germany.

Besides Morrison, hordes of newsreel cameramen and photographers were at the airfield to film the *Hindenburg* as it floated in through the cloudy sky. The *Hindenburg* was a majestic sight. It was like a huge cigar-shaped cathedral in the sky: 245 meters (800 feet) long, more than two and a half times as long as a modern jumbo jet or a football field. Up until that evening, the *Hindenburg* had safely crossed the Atlantic eighteen times, taking over 1,500 passengers in all.

Morrison was there with recording engineer Charles Neilson to describe to

The Hindenburg *airship as it comes in to land at Lakehurst, New Jersey, on May 6, 1937.*

millions of listeners the landing of the *Hindenburg* with its 36 passengers and 61 crew members. He wanted to bring the scene to life for them. He began slowly and softly setting the scene...

"It is practically standing still now. The ropes have been dropped and they have been taken hold of by a number of men on the field. It is starting to rain again. The rain has slacked up a little bit. The back motors of the ship are holding it just enough to keep it ..."

Suddenly, the people seated in front of their radios all over the United States heard him catch his breath. His voice changed; he became tense and alarmed . . .

"It's burst into flame! Get out of the way! Get this, Charley, get out of the way, please! It is bursting into flames! This is terrible! This is one of the worst **catastrophes** in the world! The flames are 500 feet into the sky. It is a terrific crash, ladies and gentlemen. It is in smoke and flames now. Oh the humanity! Those passengers!"

By now, people were tumbling out of the ship, trying to escape as the huge bags of **hydrogen** gas that kept the airship floating went up in a vast sheet of flame. The horrified Morrison was completely overcome by what he saw . . .

"I can't talk, ladies and gentlemen. Honest, it is a mass of smoking wreckage. Lady, I am sorry, honestly I can hardly . . . I am going to step inside where I can't see it. Charley, this is terrible! Listen, folks, I am going to have to stop for a minute because I have lost my voice."

Thirty-two seconds from the moment Morrison noticed the first flame coming from the *Hindenburg*'s **hull**, it was a mass of tangled steel and smoking wreckage. Thirty-five people had died. What had gone wrong?

The moment of tragedy as the airship hits
the tall mooring mast. The landing ropes
to moor the airship blow loosely in the
wind.

THE LARGEST AIRSHIP

In 1934, the Zeppelin Company began work on its 129th airship. It was named after the veteran German soldier Paul von Hindenburg, who had recently died. He was the last democratically elected president of the German Republic before Adolf Hitler and the National Socialists (Nazis) seized power.

The *Hindenburg* was over 245 meters (800 feet) long, with a diameter of 40 meters (131 feet), as high as a fifteen-story building. Its **duralumin** frame had three **catwalks** running from end to end and ladders reaching to every part of the airship, so that the crew could inspect every

inch of its structure during flight. The catwalks and ladders were covered with rubber to guard against electric sparks, which could start a fire. Its sixteen **gas bags**, or cells, contained over 198,000 cubic meters (6,992,370 cubic feet) of gas.

Despite its vast size, the *Hindenburg* was surprisingly light. The strongly built hull, with its network of girders, the envelope of fabric that covered it, the gas bags and all the internal fittings, weighed only 145 tons. This meant that the airship could carry 123 tons of passengers and mail. The motors could drive the airship at a top speed of 135 kph (84 mph). It could

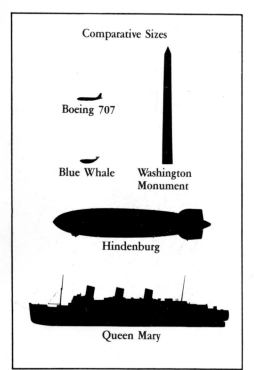

Comparative Sizes

Boeing 707

Blue Whale

Washington Monument

Hindenburg

Queen Mary

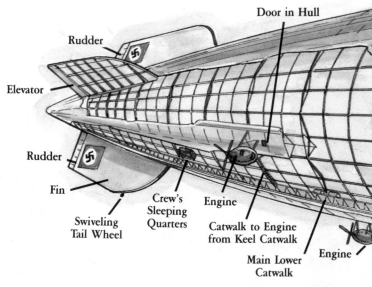

Rudder

Elevator

Rudder

Fin

Swiveling Tail Wheel

Crew's Sleeping Quarters

Engine

Door in Hull

Catwalk to Engine from Keel Catwalk

Main Lower Catwalk

Engine

cruise at 125 kph (78 mph) and had enough fuel to travel 12,000 kilometers (7,450 miles). Yet, in flight, passengers were so unaware of the noise of the motors that they could hear dogs bark on the ground 50 meters (165 feet) below.

Above *The vast size of the airship can be seen clearly in this picture.*

Below *A cut-away view of the* **Hindenburg** *showing the passenger decks, engines and catwalks.*

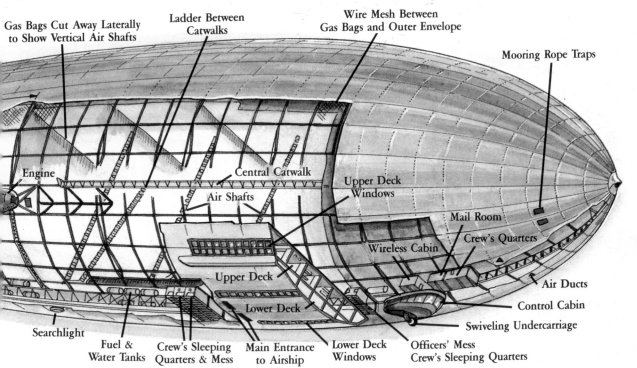

Gas Bags Cut Away Laterally to Show Vertical Air Shafts

Ladder Between Catwalks

Wire Mesh Between Gas Bags and Outer Envelope

Mooring Rope Traps

Engine

Central Catwalk

Air Shafts

Upper Deck Windows

Mail Room

Crew's Quarters

Wireless Cabin

Air Ducts

Upper Deck

Control Cabin

Lower Deck

Swiveling Undercarriage

Searchlight

Fuel & Water Tanks

Crew's Sleeping Quarters & Mess

Main Entrance to Airship

Lower Deck Windows

Officers' Mess Crew's Sleeping Quarters

The gas bags were originally intended to be filled with **helium**, which does not burn; but the United States, which held most of the world's supplies of the gas, did not trust Hitler and power-hungry Nazi Germany and did not like the idea of supplying helium to a potential enemy. So the airship had to use hydrogen, the lightest of all gases, but one that catches fire easily.

The first airships

The Zeppelin Company was founded in May 1898 by the first man to build a really practical airship, Count Ferdinand von Zeppelin. His first ship flew in 1900, and in 1910, after several setbacks, Zeppelin, aged 72, started the world's first airline. It was called *Delag*, which was short for the German words meaning *The German Airship Transportation Company*. Between

Right *The huge metal framework of the* Graf Zeppelin.

Below Left *A Zeppelin factory in Britain during World War I (1914–1918). At the table on the left, women are coating the linen fabric (which goes around the airship) with rubber. At the second table, "goldbeaters skin" – from the large intestine of the ox – is laid on the fabric to make it gas-tight.*

1910 and 1914, *Delag* carried hundreds of passengers safely all over Germany.

By the end of World War I (1914–1918) in November 1918, Germany had built nearly 100 Zeppelins and had used them to drop bombs on British and French cities. The airship had proved its use in peace and war.

Other nations also built airships. Britain abandoned its building program after the R101 airship, at that time the biggest in the world, crashed in October 1930 with only six survivors. The United States Navy used its airships *Akron* and *Macon* for **reconnaissance** purposes. Both of them also crashed; many people died in the *Akron* disaster.

Nobody, it seemed, had the skill of the Germans, and certainly nobody had their experience. In 1934, following the outstanding success of the 127th Zeppelin, built in 1926 and named after Graf (Count) Zeppelin himself, they decided to build two more airships to operate a fast and reliable service across the Atlantic to Brazil and the United States.

Fitting out

The *Hindenburg* was intended to compete with the great steamship liners that regularly crossed the Atlantic, so it was designed to carry 50 passengers in similar luxury and comfort.

It had two main passenger decks. The lower one contained the galley, where the meals were cooked on electric stoves. It also had a bar, complete with smoking saloon, kept under special pressure to prevent hydrogen from leaking in and causing a fire. It was fitted with special electric cigarette lighters (naked flames were much too dangerous). The lower deck also contained bathrooms and showers — the height of luxury air travel.

The central part of the upper deck contained the twenty-five passenger cabins. There were two passengers in each cabin, all traveling in the same class. As everything on board had to be as light as possible, the compact, softly lit cabins had foldaway aluminum washbasins with running hot and cold water, neat storage cupboards and built-in folding tables.

Below *The dining saloon on the* **Hindenburg** *was comfortable and had the most modern furniture.*

Right *A cut-away view of the passenger section of the* Hindenburg. *The steps beneath the cabins were lowered on landing for passengers to disembark.*

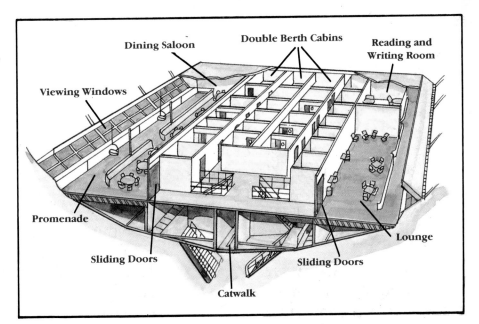

Dining Saloon

Double Berth Cabins

Reading and Writing Room

Viewing Windows

Promenade

Sliding Doors

Catwalk

Sliding Doors

Lounge

The cabins were next to the dining saloon on one side and the spacious lounge and reading room on the other. The lounge even had a lightweight aluminum grand piano! A 15-meter (50-foot) promenade deck ran along each side of the upper deck so travelers could look at the view.

The meals on board were not like the dull, tasteless "packaged" food that we often get on modern airplanes today. A typical dinner included soup, a fish course, a main dish (venison, or deer-meat, was a favorite) and a cheese dish. On each voyage, the *Hindenburg* carried 250 bottles of the best German wine. As on a luxury liner, the passengers dined in turn at the captain's table, relaxing and chatting with him as his personal guests.

Above *The* **Hindenburg** *was often described as a "floating hotel," and it had all the luxuries of the great steamship liners. This is the reading and writing room.*

The single flight to Europe for American passengers cost $400, which was what people paid for a small sedan at that time. The fare included all meals on board, sleeping accommodation and tips for the waiters and porters.

Dr. Hugo Eckener, Germany's most experienced airshipman, who had been with the Zeppelin Company since its earliest days, was pleased with the new *Hindenburg*. "At long last," he told his colleagues, "we have built a *real* airship."

The launch

By March 1936, the *Hindenburg* was ready for its first trial flights. Time was short, as it was due to make its first commercial flight to Rio de Janeiro in Brazil, on March 31.

Early that month, it was christened in the specially built hangar at the Zeppelin factory at Friedrichshafen, in southern Germany. Hitler's National Socialist government had helped to finance the new airship, and they were determined to use the *Hindenburg* for **propaganda** purposes.

Soon after the launching ceremony, and before its maiden flight, they made the crew fly the airship all over Germany, broadcasting propaganda speeches and dropping election leaflets. It was even used as a polling station, and the 104 people on board all voted for Hitler! Then it set out for Rio de Janeiro, without having undergone the full-speed trials. Eckener was furious, and with good reason.

Below *The success of the* **Hindenburg** *was used by Hitler as propaganda.*

Above *Ernst Lehmann on a previous* Hindenburg *flight.*

Left *The navigational control cabin on the airship.*

The airship nearly ran into disaster on the return flight because of trouble in two of the engines, but Eckener flew it carefully, steering into regions where he could take maximum advantage of the winds. Finally, it reached home safely. The engines were thoroughly checked, and the faulty parts replaced. In 1936, it made 16 trips across the Atlantic, six to Rio de Janeiro and ten to Lakehurst, New Jersey. An average crossing lasted less than two and a half days — half the time needed by a luxury liner for the trip.

In every respect the airship was a huge success. Because the gas bags were inflated with hydrogen rather than the heavier, but safer, helium it was designed for, state-rooms for another 20 passengers were installed for the 1937 season. This would lead to a bigger profit. Things looked bright for the Zeppelin Company — and the Nazis.

But, Eckener disliked the way the Nazis took the credit for the *Hindenburg's* success, and said so publicly. Very soon, they forced him to resign from the Zeppelin Company. He was replaced by another experienced airship captain, Ernst Lehmann.

The *Hindenburg's* first flight of 1937, to Rio de Janeiro, went well. Eighteen trips to the United States were scheduled to follow. And punctually at 8 p.m. on the evening of May 3, the airship left the new terminal at Frankfurt on what was meant to be the first of them.

THE LAST VOYAGE

After the *Hindenburg* cast off from Frankfurt that evening, it headed northward up the Rhine, passed over Cologne and then turned west down the English Channel and out into the Atlantic. It was going to cross by the shortest route, over Newfoundland in Canada, and the captain, Max Pruss, who had had 25 years experience of Zeppelins flew low so that the passengers could see the icebergs in the ocean below. One passenger, Margaret Mather, described the trip . . .

"We flew high above the storm, but a strong headwind buffeted and delayed us. It sounded like surf, but the ship sailed calmly through it . . . I told Captain Pruss how much I was enjoying the trip, and what a wretched sailor I was on the sea. He was pleased but assured me that it was one of the worst trips he had made. The wind grew stronger and the second night the captain did not go to bed at all, but still one felt no motion, though the wind beat like waves against the sides of the ship."

The strong headwinds slowed the *Hindenburg*'s progress and Pruss radioed to Lakehurst to say that he would arrive twelve hours late, at 6 p.m. on May 6.

Below *On the voyage, the captain flew low enough for the passengers to see icebergs in the ocean below.*

When the airship arrived, it was raining heavily, so Pruss waited. At 6:30 p.m. he slowly circled the airfield, and dropped the landing ropes for the landing crew to guide the airship in. The motors were switched off. The *Hindenburg* floated down toward the **mooring mast**. The time was 7:21 p.m.

The mooring crew, firefighters and onlookers rush to the scene of the tragedy to help survivors away from danger. Others stagger free in total disbelief and shock.

Disaster

Suddenly, with still 60 meters (198 feet) to go, the airship shuddered; one of the crew thought he heard a rumble like a muffled explosion. Pruss checked the instruments, but nothing seemed to be wrong.

Then a small wisp of flame appeared near the tail of the airship, just forward of the upper **fin**. There was a great roar of sound, and the horrified spectators watched helplessly as flames rapidly engulfed the tail portion of the ship. The front section, nearly 180 meters (594 feet) long, settled gently down to the ground, and the flames raced along it too. The airship tilted upward, resembling a huge chimney. A sea of flames shot upward through it for a few seconds. Then the red-hot wreckage collapsed.

Leonhard Adelt, one of the passengers on board, wrote later that all he heard was a light pop, "like a beer bottle being opened." The bow of the ship seemed to glow, as if the sun were rising behind it. Suddenly he realized that it was on fire. He glanced down to the earth and saw a sheer drop of about 40 meters (132 feet). As he was wondering whether to jump, the ship hit the ground with terrific force. Shouting to the other passengers to jump out through the observation window, he dragged his wife with him and leaped to the ground, amid a tangled mass of hot metal and clouds of burning diesel oil.

He and his wife beat a frenzied path through the flames, tearing the red-hot metal apart with their bare hands. They were so shocked at the time that they did not feel the pain. "It was like a dream," he wrote afterwards; "our bodies had no weight. They floated like stars through space."

The rescue

On board, everybody was in a frenzy, but few people had time to panic. One elderly lady walked out by the normal exit as if nothing at all had happened. Another passenger hacked his way out with his hands. A 14-year-old cabin boy leaped to the ground and was saved from the flames as a bursting **ballast** tank showered water all over him. Second cook, Alfred Groezinger, leaped 16 meters (53 feet) to safety from a window near the shower baths. Margaret Mather, sitting in a state of shock amid the flames with her coat over her head to shield her, suddenly realized that three men were beckoning to her to get out. "Aren't you coming?" one of them shouted. Groping for her handbag, she stumbled and scrambled over the bits of burning wreckage in front of her and escaped into the open air.

Others, notably twelve members of the crew on duty all over the airship waiting to guide it in, died at their posts, clinging to the girders as it collapsed in a heap of burning wreckage. Everything happened so quickly and unexpectedly that, though

on full alert, they were taken by surprise.

Friends, relatives, the 200-strong mooring party and the firefighters, standing by for just such an emergency, rushed to save as many people as they could; and miraculously, of 97 people on board, 62 survived. The deep sand on the airfield help to cushion the falls of passengers as they jumped from the burning airship. Thirteen passengers and 22 of the crew died.

The firefighters fought the blaze for three hours as the diesel fuel burned itself away. Naval first-aid crews helped beat out the flaming clothes of the survivors who staggered from the wreck. Off-duty nurses from three Lakehurst hospitals were urgently summoned by telephone. Ambulances screamed to the scene to pick up the casualties, some of whom were suffering from appalling burns.

The journalists, aware of the horror of the tragedy, made no effort to phone in their stories from the one available telephone. Instead, they all pooled their information as they collected it from the dazed survivors.

One of the victims was the previous captain of the *Hindenburg*, Ernst Lehmann. He leaped 30 meters (100 feet) from the inferno, walked calmly away from the wreck, and was rushed to hospital. He died at 6 a.m. the next day and his last words were "Ich verstehe es nicht": "I don't understand it." Nobody did.

Inset Left
Firefighters and onlookers run for cover as the airship explodes in the sky. After the explosion, they returned to help the victims.

Left *As the flames died out, the tangled wreckage could be seen.*

Right *Survivor Alfred Groezinger, cook on the airship, in the hospital.*

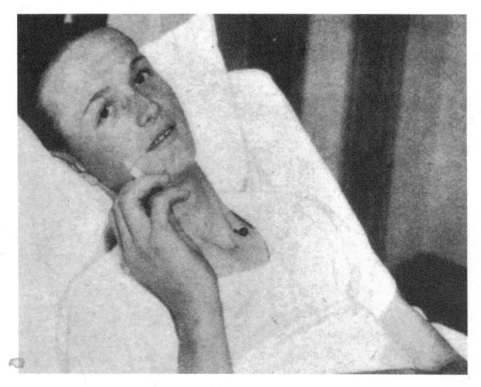

A WORLD IN SHOCK

Within minutes, the story was radioed all around the world. It became front-page news in almost every newspaper and was broadcast from a vast number of radio stations. It was even picked up by the radio officer of the *Graf Zeppelin*, flying back to Germany from Brazil. The passengers were not told about the disaster until they landed at Friedrichshafen two days later. They were among the last people in the world to learn about the crash, for everyone else already knew.

The terrible news was received not only with shock, horror and pity for the victims but also with total disbelief. Not one

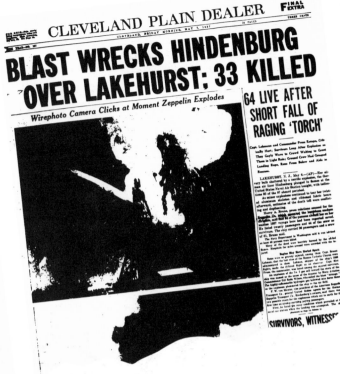

Opposite page and above American *newspaper headlines report the tragic reality of the disaster.*

passenger's life had ever been lost before in a German airship. The *Graf Zeppelin* had flown over a million kilometers (621,000 miles) and carried thousands of passengers without incident on nearly 600 flights, and that airship had not even been specially designed for the transatlantic service. How was it that the *Hindenburg*, the largest passenger-carrying vessel ever to take to the air, with every possible safety device and every detail of its cargo checked before every voyage, had gone up in flames in just half a minute?

In Germany itself, people were shocked and stunned. They also felt a sense of hurt national pride and gradually became suspicious of **sabotage**. The Nazis had many enemies, both within Germany and outside. Perhaps such enemies, wishing to discredit Hitler's evil dictatorship, had deliberately destroyed the airship in which the Nazis had taken such pride.

An inquiry was immediately ordered by the United States Department of Commerce. A three-man commission headed by South Trimble, Jr., a 40-year-old lawyer from Kentucky, began hearing the evidence just four days after the crash.

The inquiry

For eighteen days, witnesses and survivors were closely questioned. Commander Charles Rosendahl, an experienced American airship captain, who had been at Lakehurst, testified that he had seen a flame appear just forward of the rudder fin a few seconds before the explosion. Other witnesses agreed with him. Another witness added that the initial flame had burned slowly to start with, just as pure hydrogen does.

Eckener, the dismissed captain of the *Hindenburg*, flew to Cherbourg, France, on the orders of the German Air Ministry, and caught the first available liner to the United States to give his opinion. The only logical explanation he could offer was that, when the *Hindenburg* turned sharply in toward the landing mast, a **bracing wire** in the hull must have snapped, and the broken end had torn a gas bag. The escaping gas would have been ignited by **static electricity** from the sultry atmosphere following the storm.

Captain Hans von Schiller, the commander of the *Graf Zeppelin*, agreed with Eckener's theory. Neither the U.S. Department of Commerce inquiry, the U.S. Navy inquiry, nor the Gestapo (German secret police) investigation could find any evidence that the crash was other than an accident.

Others didn't accept Eckener's verdict and that of the two inquiries. They claimed that someone on board, wishing to discredit the Nazis, had placed a bomb in the frame of the airship, timed to go off

Below *An aerial view of the remains of the* Hindenburg's *tangled frame the day after the tragedy.*

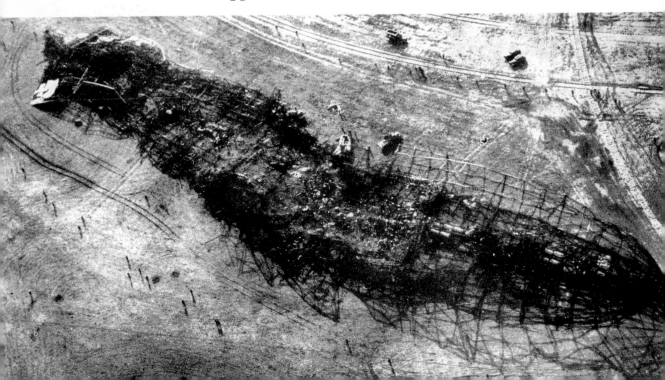

at 7:20 p.m. If the *Hindenburg* had kept to the planned schedule of arrival it would have landed at 6 p.m. and there would have been hardly anyone on board, as most people would have disembarked. That way,

Above *Step-by-step photographs of the disaster as it occurred.*

the airship would have been destroyed but few, if any, human lives lost.

END OF THE ROAD?

The loss of those 35 lives shook the Zeppelin Company's confidence in the safety of hydrogen-filled airships. Helium was essential; so, later in 1937, Eckener was sent to persuade the Americans to release enough helium for a new airship, the *LZ-130*, then being built. They agreed at first, but when Hitler invaded Austria in March 1938, the U.S. government forbade the shipment. Without helium the risks of fire were too great, and the transatlantic passenger service was abandoned.

The *Graf Zeppelin* made one more flight. *LZ-130*, now called *Graf Zeppelin II*, was completed and made about 30 flights, but it never entered passenger service. Just before World War II (1939–1945), it was sent to spy on British radar

Below *The majestic sight of the* **Graf Zeppelin** *airship (over Wembley Stadium, England, in 1930) would become a thing of the past. In 1939, German airships were destroyed on the orders of Goering.*

defenses. However, when war broke out, the *Graf Zeppelin*, *Graf Zeppelin II*, and the huge airship sheds at Frankfurt were blown up on the orders of Goering, the chief of the **Luftwaffe**. It was the end of the Zeppelins.

The future lay with the airplane. Early commercial airplanes could not match the flying time or load **capacity** of airships like the *Hindenburg*. But, by 1939, airplanes were built capable of taking thirty passengers over 1,000 kilometers (621 miles) nonstop. Airplanes could be built much faster than airships, too. During World War II, thousands were built

Above *The* **Graf Zeppelin** *moored in Recife, Brazil. It made only one more flight after the* **Hindenburg** *disaster. The days of the rigid airships were over.*

to carry soldiers and heavy equipment.

When the war ended in 1945, civil aviation developed very quickly. First the **turboprop** and then the jet engine vastly improved the performance of airplanes. An airplane flying at 500 kph (310 mph) could make five times as many journeys in a given time as an airship flying at 100 kph (62 mph). But the airship refused to die.

27

The future

In 1947, Eckener and the American Goodyear Corporation drew up plans for an airship 300 meters (990 feet) long and capable of taking 232 passengers for 10,000 kilometers (6,210 miles) at 150 kph (93 mph). Neither industry nor the U.S. government was interested in their idea. The competition from airplanes was too strong. By 1948, airplanes like the DC6 could carry 70 passengers at 450 kph (279 mph), and in the 1950s the pioneer jet plane, the De Havilland *Comet*, could take a similar load at over 800 kph (497 mph). Obviously the **rigid airship** was no competitor to the jet airplane.

Yet the airship may still have a future. The early pre-Zeppelin type of airship can still be seen from time to time flying over Britain and the United States today. The modern **blimp**, as it is sometimes called, has only one huge gas bag and needs no frame to support it. During both world wars, blimps were used on antisubmarine and mine-sweeping patrols with great success, and the American Goodyear Company has continued making them up until the present.

Below *Airplanes like the* Comet *could carry as great a load as airships and traveled faster.*

The modern plastic materials, which are much stronger than the fabrics of the Zeppelin gas bags, enable really large bags to be used. Modern bonding techniques also mean that the engine and passenger areas can be much more firmly fixed to the gas bag. Thus all the weight and cost of a supporting metal frame can be avoided.

Moreover, though speed is on the airplane's side, other factors are not. Modern jets cost a lot to build and maintain. The pollution and noise they cause is another disadvantage. Long runways are needed for take-off and landing, whereas an airship needs only a large field to land in, with a mooring mast. There is far more room in an airship's cabin than in the cramped cabin of even a jumbo jet.

Above *The Goodyear Company's airship today. Airships are used successfully for advertising.*

Although airships as yet have not re-emerged as commercial passenger transportation, large companies have not been slow to realize the spectacular advertising potential of an airship. A huge advertisement on the side of an airship floating serenely over a large town can reach thousands of people at one time. Because they can fly quite slowly, airships are also as effective as helicopters in making scientific surveys, and they are more comfortable.

So, though the great rigid airships, so grand and so majestic, are a thing of the past, there may still be a place for the **non-rigid airship** in the 21st century.

GLOSSARY

Ballast Extra weight (usually in the form of water in the case of airships) carried deliberately to balance the ship and ensure that it could quickly lighten itself if the air pressure suddenly dropped and the airship began to lose height.

Blimp *see* Nonrigid airship.

Bracing wire Wire used to strengthen the metal frame of a Zeppelin-type of airship.

Capacity The amount that something can carry or hold.

Catastrophe A sudden disaster.

Catwalks Long, narrow pathways or corridors.

Duralumin A light, strong aluminum alloy (mixture) containing 3.5 – 4.5 percent of copper with small quantities of silicon, magnesium and manganese. Used a great deal in aircraft manufacture.

Fin The fins of an airship, usually fixed to the stern of the ship's hull, served to keep it from rolling from side to side and had the elevators and rudder attached to them so that the ship could be steered, raised and lowered in flight.

Gas bag (gas cell) The huge balloonlike structures inside the frame of an airship that gave it lift. In the *Hindenburg* there were 16 of them.

Helium The second lightest element. It is a very rare gas, (most of the world's helium is found in the United States and the USSR), and an artificial substitute cannot easily be made. Twice as heavy as hydrogen, but much lighter than air, it has the great advantage over hydrogen in that it will not burn.

Hull The main body of an airship.

Hydrogen The lightest known element. It can be easily produced in large quantities, but it is very dangerous as it burns very readily.

Luftwaffe, the The German air force under the Nazis.

Mooring mast Because airships were so huge, it became the custom to moor them by the pointed front end to stoutly built masts, so the ship could continue to float in the air.

Nonrigid airship An airship without a metal frame to support the envelope of canvas that protects the gas cells from the elements. Such an airship is lighter and much simpler to build.

Propaganda The spreading of ideas and information purposely to make others accept them. The word now suggests that the information is false or misleading.

Reconnaissance The act of gathering information or spying on the position and activities of an enemy.

Rigid airship   An airship in which the gas cells are enclosed within, and attached to, a strong metal frame. Over this frame is stretched an envelope (usually of canvas) to protect the gas cells from damage. The *Hindenburg* was a rigid airship.

Sabotage   To deliberately damage or destroy a piece of equipment or machine.

Static electricity   Natural electricity in the atmosphere; it is harmless until it encounters a conductor that provides a route for it to the earth.

Turboprop   A gas turbine for driving an aircraft propeller.

BOOKS TO READ

The Airship Ladyship Adventure (fiction), Jonathan Gathorne-Hardys. Lippincott Jr. Books, 1977

Balloons, Zeppelins & Dirigibles, Aaron W. Perceful. Franklin Watts, 1983

Dirigible, Joshua Stoff. Macmillan, 1985

My Zeppelins, Hugo Eckener (translated by Douglas Robinson). Ayer Co., 1979

FURTHER INFORMATION

See if you can find any newspapers or magazines of the time that reported the *Hindenburg* disaster. Your local library might be able to help you. Eyewitness accounts are also very interesting, as they give an idea of what it must have been like to travel on the *Hindenburg*, and give you personal accounts of the tragedy itself. Your library may have a copy of the original radio news broadcast on an LP record. Perhaps it's available on casset, too. One LP record of the original broadcast is: "The Last Flight of the Hindenburg," A George Garabedian Production, 1974, Mark 56 Records, Anaheim, CA 92805.

Index

ACKNOWLEDGMENTS

The publishers would like to thank the following for providing the photographs in this book:
BBC Hulton Picture Library 10, 15, 21; Goodyear International 29; John Frost Historical
Newspapers 22-23; The Mansell Collection 9 (above), 11, 14, 16 (left); Topham Picture Library
6, 16 (right), 20 (both), 24, 25, 26, 27. The illustrations on pages 8-9 and page 13 are by Stephen
Wheele.